Landmark
Events in
American
History

# The Writing of "The Star-Spangled Banner"

Scott Ingram

**WORLD ALMANAC® LIBRARY**

Please visit our web site at: www.worldalmanaclibrary.com
For a free color catalog describing World Almanac® Library's list of high-quality
books and multimedia programs, call 1-800-848-2928 (USA) or 1-800-387-3178
(Canada). World Almanac® Library's fax: (414) 332-3567.

**Library of Congress Cataloging-in-Publication Data**

Ingram, Scott (William Scott).
    The writing of "The Star-Spangled Banner" / by Scott Ingram.
      p. cm. — (Landmark events in American history)
    Includes bibliographical references and index.
    Contents: Trouble at sea — The war hawks — The War of 1812 begins —
Chesapeake Bay — Attack on Fort McHenry — The final months.
    ISBN 0-8368-5390-3 (lib. bdg.)
    ISBN 0-8368-5418-7 (softcover)
    1. Baltimore, Battle of, Baltimore, Md., 1814—Juvenile literature. 2. United States—
History—War of 1812—Flags—Juvenile literature. 3. Flags—United States—History—
19th century—Juvenile literature. 4. Key, Francis Scott, 1779-1843—Juvenile
literature. 5. Star-spangled banner (Song)—Juvenile literature. [1. Baltimore, Battle of,
Baltimore, Md., 1814. 2. United States—History—War of 1812. 3. Flags—United
States—History. 4. Key, Francis Scott, 1779-1843. 5. Star-spangled banner (Song).]
    I. Title. II. Series.
    E356.B2I54   2004
    782.4215'99'0973—dc22                      2003061384

First published in 2004 by
**World Almanac® Library**
330 West Olive Street, Suite 100
Milwaukee, WI 53212 USA

Copyright © 2004 by World Almanac® Library.

Produced by Discovery Books
Editor: Sabrina Crewe
Designer and page production: Sabine Beaupré
Photo researcher: Sabrina Crewe
Maps and diagrams: Stefan Chabluk
World Almanac® Library editorial direction: Mark J. Sachner
World Almanac® Library art direction: Tammy Gruenewald
World Almanac® Library production: Jessica Morris

Photo credits: American Antiquarian Society: p. 32; Corbis: cover, pp. 4, 6, 7, 14, 18,
22, 23, 25, 26, 27, 29, 31, 33, 34, 36, 39, 42; Maryland Historical Society: pp. 5, 35;
North Wind Picture Archives: pp. 8, 9, 10, 12, 13, 15, 16, 17, 19, 20, 24, 28, 40, 41;
Smithsonian Institution National Museum of American History: p. 43.

Printed in the United States of America

1 2 3 4 5 6 7 8 9 08 07 06 05 04

# Contents

# Introduction

### The British Attack Begins

Heavy rain fell on Fort McHenry in the second week of September 1814. The star-shaped fort lay in Chesapeake Bay, at the southern end of the Patapsco River. Its job was to protect the busy port of Baltimore, Maryland, from the British army.

Britain had been at war with the United States for two years in a conflict now known as the War of 1812. Battles had been fought from **U.S. territories** of the Northwest into Canada, and the British had blockaded some U.S. ports.

By early September, more than thirty British ships lay in the Patapsco River. On September 13, 1814, the cannons of the British ships began firing exploding **shells** toward Fort McHenry from about two miles (3 kilometers) down river.

### Under Siege

The bombardment continued for more than twenty-four hours. Despite the fearsome display of British firepower, the Americans inside the fort held their ground. In a later report, Fort McHenry's commander, Major George Armistead, wrote that despite "a constant and tremendous shower of shells . . . not a man shrunk from the conflict."

### The Writing of a Song

Several miles down the Patapsco River, an American lawyer named Francis Scott Key heard the bombardment. On the morning of September 14, as the sounds of **artillery** ceased, Key sailed toward Fort McHenry, expecting the worst. There, waving in the morning light, was a huge United States flag. Inspired by the sight, Key composed part of a poem on the back of a letter. The words became the lyrics to "The Star Spangled Banner," a patriotic song later chosen as the U.S. national anthem. Because of the song, the defense of Fort McHenry will always be remembered in U.S. history.

## An Important Battle

The attack on and defense of the fort—known as the Battle of Baltimore—was significant for another reason. The loss of Baltimore could well have spelled defeat for the young United States. By withstanding the British bombardment, however, the soldiers at Fort McHenry were able to disrupt the timing of land and sea attacks by the British on Baltimore. The invading force had to retreat from Chesapeake Bay and, soon afterward, from U.S. territory farther north as well.

**Words From the Heart**

"Then, in that hour of deliverance, my heart spoke. Does not such a country, and such defenders of their country, deserve a song?"

*Francis Scott Key, 1814*

Veterans of the Battle of Baltimore gathered on Defenders' Day, celebrated every year in Baltimore on September 12. This photograph of the defenders was taken in 1880.

# Trouble at Sea

In 1803, Thomas Jefferson (seated at desk) signed the document in which the United States agreed to buy the vast Louisiana Territory from France.

## Jefferson's First Term

The events that led up to the Battle of Baltimore in 1814 had begun in the previous decade, during the period (1801–1809) when Thomas Jefferson was president. The first years of Jefferson's term in office were among the most successful of any U.S. president in **economic** terms. Not only did **foreign trade** double, but the nation's debt was reduced by many millions.

## Competing Laws

U.S. economic fortunes changed, however, in 1806, when Britain and France began stepping up their interference with U.S. trade. In November 1807, Britain issued Orders in Council, an order banning all **merchant ships** from trading in ports under French control in Europe. The new law meant that all merchant ships in the Atlantic Ocean had to stop at British ports instead. Those that did not comply would be stopped at sea, and their cargo would be seized.

Upon learning of the British law, the French leader Napoleon Bonaparte issued the Milan Decree in December 1807. Under this declaration, merchant ships that obeyed the Orders in Council, or allowed the British navy to stop them on the high seas, could be seized by France.

## American Ships Suffer

To enforce these contradictory orders, French and British naval ships patrolled the open oceans in an attempt to keep trade vessels out of each other's ports. The vessels that got the worst of this conflict on the oceans were American merchant ships. An American

Until the early 1800s, both France and Britain had interests in North America. France had controlled the enormous Louisiana Territory west of the Mississippi River until 1803, when it sold the land to the United States. Britain had given up its colonies in the East after the American Revolution, but still controlled Canada and several islands in the West Indies.

The United States was important to both Britain and France. U.S. ships were considered among the best vessels on the ocean and were the main carriers of goods from the Americas, the West Indies, and even Asia. In addition, raw materials from North America, such as lumber and cotton, were impor-

The Napoleonic Wars were named for Emperor Napoleon Bonaparte of France, above, who aimed to conquer Europe.

tant to both powers. So, too, were food products such as beef, pork, and grain.

For long periods between 1793 and 1814, Britain and France were at war with each other in the Napoleonic Wars. In the course of the conflict, the French gained control of most of Europe, while Britain's powerful navy retained control of the seas. The war became a stalemate, and with little hope of military triumph, the two powers decided to attack each other's economies. One way to do this was to interfere with the vital shipping and trade that stemmed from the United States and the rest of North America.

ship sailing to a port under French control could be seized by a British ship if it had not stopped first at a British port. Any American ship that made such a stop, however, could be seized by a French naval vessel.

# Impressment

No practice infuriated the American public more in the early 1800s than the British policy of impressment. This form of kidnapping involved the forcible removal of U.S. sailors from their ships to serve on British vessels.

Conditions for sailors in the British navy were notoriously poor. Pay was low, less than half of that on U.S. merchant ships. In addition, British naval discipline was brutal, and living conditions were intolerable. As a result, British sailors often deserted the British navy to serve on American merchant ships.

Due to the desertions, British commanders began to stop and board U.S. ships on the open seas in search of British sailors. In the process, many Americans were forced, or "impressed," into the British navy under false charges that they were British deserters.

Americans were outraged when the British navy refused to stop impressing U.S. sailors. Thousands of American men were impressed in the early 1800s.

In June 1807, the British boarded the USS *Chesapeake* and demanded its surrender. This picture shows the *Chesapeake*'s commander surrendering his sword.

## The *Chesapeake* Affair

More than nine hundred U.S. ships were seized by the British and French in the years between 1807 and 1812, greatly damaging the U.S. economy. One event, involving the unpopular British practice of impressment, focused Americans' anger firmly on Britain, even before the Orders in Council had been issued.

The USS *Chesapeake* was a naval gunboat that left the United States in June 1807, headed for the Mediterranean Sea. The warship's mission was to protect U.S. merchant ships. Shortly after reaching the open sea, the *Chesapeake* encountered the British warship *Leopard*. The British ship, by signaling that it had a message, fooled the *Chesapeake* into slowing. The *Leopard* then pulled alongside the U.S. ship and demanded the right to search for British deserters. When the U.S. commander refused, the *Leopard* opened fire, killing three U.S. sailors and wounding eighteen. British sailors then boarded the *Chesapeake* and took four men they claimed were deserters. The helpless *Chesapeake* was forced to return to the United States.

**Outrage on the *Chesapeake***
"We will be universally justified in the eyes of the world, and unanimously supported by the nation, if the ground of war be England's refusal to disavow or to make satisfaction for the outrage on the *Chesapeake*."

*Thomas Jefferson, journal entry regarding the* Chesapeake, *1807*

The *Chesapeake* Affair, as it was known, so enraged the American public that Jefferson knew a declaration of war would have enormous public support. He also knew, however, that the U.S. Army and Navy were no match for the British military. Instead of declaring war, he ordered all British warships to stay out of U.S. waters. Jefferson also told his ambassador in Britain to demand an apology from the British **Parliament**. Parliament responded by relieving the captain of the *Leopard* of his command.

## The Embargo Act

The British refused, however, to stop the impressment of U.S. sailors, and Jefferson realized that this practice was still a serious problem. In December 1807, Congress passed the **Embargo** Act, which not only closed U.S. ports to foreign ships, but prevented U.S. ships from sailing to foreign ports.

The Embargo Act was not popular in the United States. This cartoon shows a tobacco exporter caught in the act of smuggling barrels of tobacco to British ships because he wasn't allowed to sell his goods legally.

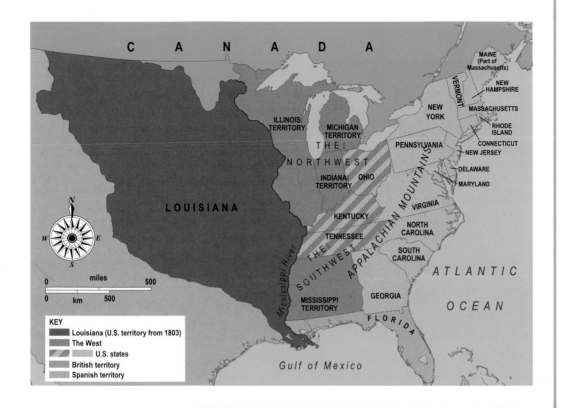

As the 1800s progressed, white settlers from the United States were expanding beyond the original thirteen states. People in the Northwest thought British Canada, like Louisiana, should be U.S. territory.

# Expanding U.S. Borders

Besides impressment and damage to U.S. shipping and trade, Americans had another reason to resent Britain: its continued control over territory in North America. Many in the United States were seeking to expand their nation's borders and take over other parts of North America for settlement. U.S. settlers had already begun to move from the eastern states into an area then known as "the **West**." By 1810, Ohio had a population of more than 200,000, more than 400,000 people were living in Kentucky, and there were almost as many in Tennessee. In addition, settlers were pushing into Indiana and Illinois from Ohio. As they pressed further west and north, many white Americans turned their eyes toward British Canada. The beginnings of a movement arose in the **Northwest** to drive Britain out of Canada and take possession of that northern land for the United States.

# The War Hawks

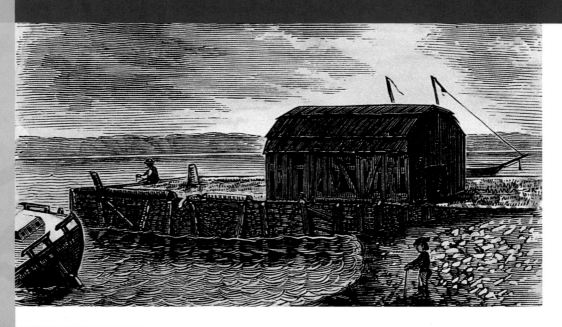

An abandoned dock with grass growing on it shows the results of the Embargo Act. Everyone from sailors to farmers suffered when U.S. foreign trade was banned.

**Error Acknowledged**

"After depriving government of its means of support for sixteen months, and preventing the people of the United States from pursuing a lawful and profitable commerce, and reducing the whole country to a state of wretchedness and poverty, our infatuated rulers, blinded by a corrupt [preference] for France, have been forced to acknowledge their fatal error, and so far to retrace their steps."

Federal Republican *newspaper,*
*March 1, 1809, regarding the repeal*
*of the Embargo Act*

## A New President and a New Law

In 1809, Congress **repealed** the Embargo Act because it was hurting the U.S. economy more than it was harming the economies of France and Britain. U.S. goods were sitting in warehouses. Crops were rotting. Sailors, dockworkers, and laborers were out of work.

In 1810, Congress replaced the Embargo Act with a law—called "Macon's Bill No. 2" after Nathaniel Macon who introduced it—that opened U.S. trade to all nations. Under the law, if either France or Britain ceased its harassment of U.S. shipping, the president could cut off trade with the other power in return.

## Napoleon's Offer

In 1809, James Madison succeeded Jefferson as president. In late 1810, Napoleon informed Madison that he would order French ships to stop seizing U.S. vessels if Madison stopped all trade with Britain. Madison was eager to use economic

## James Madison (1751—1836)

James Madison was born in Virginia, the eldest of ten children. In 1769, he enrolled in the College of New Jersey, now Princeton University. During the American Revolution, he served in the Virginia legislature.

Madison's most important role in history was his contribution to shaping the basic government and laws of the United States. He was among the delegates to the Constitutional Convention of 1787, at which the U.S. Constitution was written. Its wording was guided significantly by Madison's firm beliefs about government. Madison also wrote the Bill of Rights, the first ten amendments to the Constitution.

In 1794, while serving in Congress, Madison married Dolley Payne Todd. He became president in 1809. When his presidency ended in 1817, Madison retired to his home in Virginia, where he remained active in state politics for many years.

force against Britain, and he accepted the French offer, hoping the British would be forced to change their policy. But the French continued to seize U.S. ships, and so did the British.

### The War Hawks

In addition to foreign problems, Madison faced pressure from members of Congress from the South and West. These members, known as the War Hawks, had a firm belief in the right of U.S. citizens to take any and all lands in North America. This included not only the traditional homelands of Native Americans, but British-claimed territory in Canada.

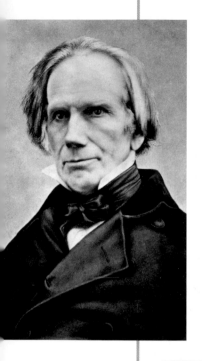

In 1811, led by Speaker of the House Henry Clay, the War Hawks made fierce speeches calling for an invasion of Canada. The War Hawks claimed that the British there were helping Native American tribes to attack U.S. settlers who had made their homes along the **frontier** in the North.

## Opposing Interests

Despite widespread anger at impressment and other issues, not all Americans supported the views of the War Hawks. Many of those who opposed the idea of war were from the Northeast. Their wealth depended on manufacture and trade, and they feared that a war would do even more harm to their economy. Madison was soon trapped between congressional representatives from the South and West, who generally supported war, and those from the East, who opposed it.

Leader of the War Hawks, Henry Clay was a powerful force in U.S. politics for many years. He was secretary of state from 1825 to 1829 and was still active in Congress in 1850.

## Tensions on the Frontier

The conflict between Native Americans and U.S. settlers had been almost constant in the first decade of the 1800s, as more and more white settlers moved into western territories. The governors of those territories aggressively attempted to convince Native American peoples to sell their lands. Between 1802 and 1805, some Native groups living in the areas that are now Indiana, Wisconsin, Missouri, and Illinois were tricked into selling their land. Others were forcibly removed.

Bitter feelings grew on both sides. For the British in Canada, the Indians' hostility to Americans was a convenient circumstance rather than a deliberate plan, as the War Hawks claimed. But the British did provide food, clothing, and weapons to Native Americans in an attempt to support the tribes and so prevent U.S. expansion into Canada. And as the tension and violence increased, Americans saw the British presence on the frontier as a challenge to U.S. independence.

Settlers in the Northwest, such as this family in Ohio, supported the War Hawks because they believed in expanding U.S. territory in North America.

The War Hawks helped spread a wave of anti-British feeling across the country. They persuaded people that the British were arming Native Americans for attacks against settlers. They also claimed the right of the United States to expand into Canada and even talked about taking control of Florida from Spain. Not surprisingly, these ideas appealed to the War Hawks' southern and western supporters, who were hungry for more land.

## Resistance to White Settlement

From the early 1800s, a Shawnee military leader, Tecumseh, had attempted to form a **confederation** of separate tribes from all over the West. Only by cooperation, said Tecumseh, could the Native

**The Right of Occupancy**

"The white people have no right to take the land from the Indians, because they had it first; it is theirs. They may sell, but all must join. . . . The late sale is bad. It was made by a part only. . . . All red men have equal rights to the unoccupied land. The right of occupancy . . . belongs to the first who sits down on his blanket or skins which he has thrown upon the ground; and till he leaves it no other has a right."

*Letter from Tecumseh to William Henry Harrison, 1811*

peoples prevent their lands from falling into the hands of white settlers. Tecumseh's brother Tenskwatawa, meanwhile, encouraged the tribes of the Northwest to keep their culture alive in the face of white settlement on Native homelands. In 1808, the brothers and their followers established a settlement called Prophetstown at the junction of the Tippecanoe and Wabash Rivers in the Indiana Territory.

Tecumseh confronts William Henry Harrison, governor of Indiana, about white settlement on Native homelands.

## The Battle of Tippecanoe

In November 1811, Tecumseh was away in the Southwest, trying to get support for the confederation. The military governor of the Indiana Territory, William Henry Harrison, marched towards Prophetstown with a thousand soldiers. His presence was intended more as a show of force than as an actual attack.

Inside Prophetstown, however, Tenskwatawa was convinced that Harrison would attack and ordered his men to make the first move. On November 7, the Battle of Tippecanoe began with a surprise attack that inflicted heavy casualties on Harrison's force. Eventually, the Native fighters ran out of gunpowder and withdrew.

The next day, Harrison's force attacked Prophetstown, which had been abandoned, and burned it to the ground.

## Madison Responds

Native resistance in the Northwest continued, and the War Hawks continued to demand a response. On June 1, 1812, President Madison sent a document to Congress that listed U.S. grievances against Britain. The list mentioned impressment, the searching of U.S. vessels in U.S. waters, embargoes that harmed the U.S. economy, and the alliance between Native Americans and the British army.

However reluctant on the president's part, it was a call to war. On June 18, 1812, Congress declared war on Britain. One month earlier, the British Parliament had revoked the Orders in Council, one of the main causes of conflict in the first place. By the time this news reached the U.S., however, the Americans felt it was too late to pull back.

On November 7, 1811, U.S. forces defeated Tenskwatawa's warriors in the Battle of Tippecanoe. The conflict is sometimes described as the first battle of the War of 1812.

**Dreaded Enemy**
"Of all the enemies to [the] public . . . war, is, perhaps, the most to be dreaded."

*James Madison, Political Observations, 1795*

17

# The War of 1812 Begins

General William Hull surrenders Fort Detroit to the British in August 1812. The United States tried Hull for treason for failing to defend U.S. territory in the Northwest. He became the only American general ever sentenced to death. Because he was over sixty, however, the sentence was never carried out.

## Canada as the Goal

In some ways, the War of 1812 was actually two wars. Although the main force behind the war was the British actions at sea, the war was first fought on the northwest frontier and across the Canadian border. In fact, the first military goal of the Americans was driving the British from Canada. The British, on the other hand, hoped to hold off the U.S. invasion until the bulk of their forces could win the war in Europe and then be sent to reinforce Canada.

Many War Hawks believed that the United States would easily win control of the lightly populated area to the north. The U.S. population was more than ten times that of Canada. But the United States was not prepared for war. There were fewer than 7,000 soldiers in the U.S. Army, and they were opposed by more than 8,500 British troops and more than 3,000 warriors from Tecumseh's confederation. The many **militia** units in states and territories were largely untrained and were little use as fighting forces.

## Early Defeats

By early summer of 1812, William Hull, the U.S. military commander in the Northwest, assembled a force of militia and regular troops for an invasion of Canada. The force marched across the border and won several small victories. When Hull learned that Tecumseh had joined forces with the British, however, he decided to return to his base at Fort Detroit, in present-day Michigan, in early August.

Two weeks later, Fort Detroit was surrounded by British and Native Americans. Hull panicked and surrendered, only to discover later that his force of 2,200 men was not only much larger than the enemy force, it was better-armed. By the end of August 1812, Americans had also surrendered forts at Mackinac and Dearborn (now Chicago). These humiliating losses meant that the British were in charge of the most of the Northwest.

Native military forces attack U.S. Fort Dearborn, at the site of present-day Chicago, in August 1812. Relations between whites and Indians in the area were very poor due to brutal U.S. campaigns the year before, and the Indians killed not just soldiers but women and children, too.

## Harrison Takes Command

In January 1813, President Madison appointed William Henry Harrison to command the Army of the Northwest. His task was to recapture the numerous forts and other outposts that had fallen to the British over the disastrous summer of 1812. However, the new year began badly. A U.S. force was defeated in the Battle of

During the War of 1812, Sackett's Harbor on Lake Ontario became a shipbuilding center. Over the course of the war, it built more vessels than any other shipyard in the United States.

Frenchtown in Michigan. In that defeat, Native Americans killed more than thirty U.S. prisoners in what became known as the Raisin River Massacre.

## War on the Great Lakes

Meanwhile, a great deal of activity took place along the border around the Great Lakes. Sackett's Harbor, an important U.S. base, was a short distance by water from the British stronghold of Kingston. The Americans planned to attack Kingston when the

## The Trek to Kingston

One important British location in the Great Lakes area was Fort Kingston on Lake Ontario, which stood directly across from the U.S. shipyards at Sackett's Harbor. In 1813, spies reported to the British that the Americans were preparing to attack Kingston when spring arrived. Unfortunately for the British, the only reinforcements were 700 miles (1,100 km) away, in Fredericton, New Brunswick. In late January 1813, British officer Lieutenant John Le Couteur received orders to march his unit of 550 men from Fredericton to Kingston. This meant traveling hundreds of miles of wilderness in the dead of winter. On February 5, Le Couteur's force set off. The men marched through temperatures of -13 to -27°F (-25 to -33°C). Incredibly, they covered the distance in an astonishing fifty-two days without the loss of a single soldier. The arrival of the heroic reinforcements in Kingston prevented a U.S. attack.

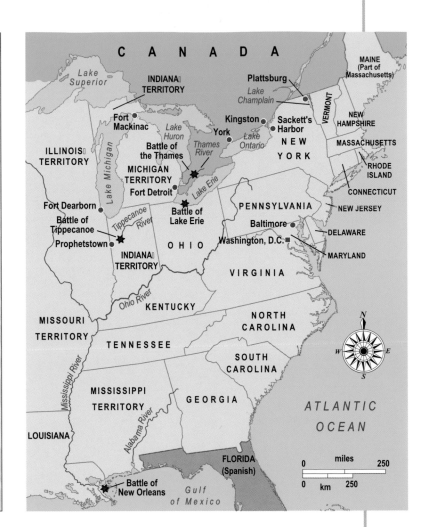

winter ice melted. Word of the U.S. plans reached the British, however, and Kingston was reinforced. As a result, the Americans turned their attention to the town of York (now Toronto), which was then the capital of Canada.

## The Attack on York

On April 27, 1813, U.S. ships ferried about 1,700 men across Lake Ontario to attack York. As U.S. forces advanced, a British gunpowder supply exploded, killing and injuring more than two hundred Americans. The U.S. commander, General Zebulon Pike, was wounded and died within hours.

British troops abandoned the town after the explosion. Without a commander, the U.S. troops ran wild, looting and burning York's public buildings as well as private homes. This act of destruction infuriated the British and would lead them to seek revenge the following year.

Much of the War of 1812 was concentrated in the Northwest and around the Great Lakes. Although U.S. land forces suffered many defeats, the nation's small navy did well from the start.

U.S. commander Oliver Perry continued to lead the Battle of Lake Erie even after his own ship was destroyed. He was rowed to another ship, and went on to win the battle and take control of the lake.

### Perry's Victory

By September 1813, the U.S. Navy controlled much of Lake Ontario and Lake Erie. The U.S. commander, Oliver Hazard Perry, had **blockaded** British ships in several harbors. British supplies were dangerously low. The British **fleet** was forced to attempt to break the U.S. blockade.

On September 10, British ships met Perry's fleet at the island of Put in Bay in the Battle of Lake Erie. After almost four hours of intense cannon fire, the British surrendered. It was the first time in history that an entire British fleet was defeated and captured by the enemy. After the battle, Perry wrote a now-famous message: "We have met the enemy and they are ours."

## The Death of Tecumseh

By October 1813, U.S. victories at York and on Lake Erie had forced the British—together with a Native army under Tecumseh—to retreat from forts along the U.S.-Canada border. They were pursued by a large force led by William Henry Harrison. Eventually, the British and Indian armies decided to face the Americans, not far from Fort Detroit.

The resulting fight was called the Battle of the Thames after a river near the battlefield. The U.S. troops defeated the British-Native American force on October 5, 1813. It was the first major land victory of the war for the United States. The battle was most notable, however, for the heroic death of Tecumseh. As British forces retreated, Tecumseh's army stood its ground, and the widely respected leader was killed in hand-to-hand combat with Kentucky militia. His death effectively ended the Native American alliance as a fighting force. With the collapse of the alliance, the land Tecumseh fought so hard to protect was opened for white settlement.

Tecumseh is shot at the Battle of the Thames.

**Die Like a Hero**

"When it comes your time to die, be not like those whose hearts are filled with . . . fear . . . so that . . . they weep and pray . . . to live their lives over again in a different way. Sing your death song and die like a hero going home."

*Tecumseh*

# Chesapeake Bay

British ships form a blockade in Chesapeake Bay during the War of 1812. Their presence stopped U.S. warships from sailing and prevented supplies from entering and leaving the ports.

**Not Coming**

"They certainly will not come here . . . What will they do here? Baltimore is . . . of so much more consequence."

*Secretary of War John Armstrong, who did not believe that the British would attack Washington, D.C., and so failed to defend the city, 1814*

## The Situation Gets Worse

Even after several victories in 1813, the United States had not established control over Canada, and many Americans were becoming disillusioned with the war. One newspaper called the War of 1812 "an unbroken series of disasters, disgrace, ruin and death." To make matters worse, a British blockade along the East coast was strangling the United States. Things looked even more bleak for the United States in the spring of 1814: Britain finally defeated France in the long war in Europe, freeing more forces for the conflict in North America. By June, a fleet of warships carrying more than fifteen thousand battle-tested troops was headed across the Atlantic.

## British Strategy

The British sent forces to three locations—Lake Champlain, the mouth of the Mississippi River, and Chesapeake Bay. Their strategy was to force U.S. troops to defend critical points within U.S. borders, but the British wanted to invade Chesapeake Bay for another reason: revenge. They planned to destroy Washington, D.C., to retaliate for the burning of the Canadian capital at York.

From the U.S. capital, the British planned to attack Baltimore, Maryland, in northwestern Chesapeake Bay. **Privateers** from Baltimore caused a

## Chesapeake Bay

Until white settlers arrived in the 1600s, many Native American groups in what is now Virginia lived around a large **estuary** they called "Cheerio," or "great shellfish bay." Chesapeake Bay is about 200 miles (320 km) long with its northern end in Maryland and its mouth at Norfolk, Virginia. It varies in width from 3 miles (4.8 km) in the north to 35 miles (56 km) in the south. The bay receives the waters of 150 major rivers and more than 100,000 streams. It is relatively shallow, with an average depth of about 21 feet (6.4 meters). This fact made it difficult for large, heavily armored British warships to sail into certain areas of the bay during the invasion of 1814.

An aerial view of part of Chesapeake Bay today shows how streams and rivers interrupt its rambling shore. The shoreline is so long that it exceeds that of the entire west coast of the United States.

great deal of disruption to British trade, having captured over 30 percent of all British ships taken during the war. To the British, Baltimore was nothing more than "a nest of pirates."

### Landing in Maryland

On August 19, 1814, a force of almost 4,500 British soldiers sailed up Chesapeake Bay and landed at the town of Benedict, Maryland, on the Patuxent River. From there, the troops marched northwest to Washington, D.C., about 60 miles (100 km) away.

When he received news of the British landing, John Armstrong, the U.S. secretary of war, hurriedly called up local militia units. Within days, more than 9,000 militia and regular troops were preparing to take on the British. Armstrong sent 5,000 men to Baltimore and ordered the remaining troops to dig defensive positions

## Sound of the Cannon

"Will you believe it, my sister? We have had a battle, or skirmish, near Bladensburg, and here I am still, within sound of the cannon! Mr. Madison comes not. May God protect us! "

*Dolley Madison, in a letter to her sister as the British approached Washington, August 24, 1814*

at the town of Bladensburg, to stop the British advance.

It was at Bladensburg that the two forces collided on August 24, 1814. Among the U.S. militia officers in charge of positioning the troops and artillery was a lawyer from nearby Georgetown named Francis Scott Key.

## The British in Washington, D.C.

Like many other militia officers, Key had no military experience. The Battle of Bladensburg was one of the most humiliating U.S. defeats in the war. British troops quickly overwhelmed the American resistance and reached Washington, D.C., by the evening of

The British set fires all over Washington, D.C., in August 1814. The city burned for two days.

## Saving the National Treasures

Dolley Madison became first lady in 1809 and was a popular hostess. She is mainly remembered today for her courage during the British invasion of Washington, D.C. When the Battle of Bladensburg began, the president and other officials fled to Georgetown. As the British army approached Washington, D.C., the militia at the presidential mansion also fled. First Lady Dolley Madison, however, refused to leave until she had packed up a prized portrait of George Washington and a copy of the Declaration of Independence. With those items safe, she escaped, leaving her own possessions behind. That evening, while British soldiers ransacked the president's mansion and Washington burned, the president and his wife searched for each other among crowds and chaos. The two eventually found each other at a roadside tavern in Georgetown.

August 24. After setting fire to several private homes, British troops invaded the stone Capitol building. There they piled up shutters and doors, added gunpowder to the wood, and started a huge bonfire. The Treasury building was burned next. From there, the troops invaded the president's mansion—known today as the White House—and ransacked and burned it.

# Attack on Fort McHenry

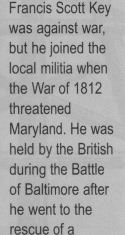

Francis Scott Key was against war, but he joined the local militia when the War of 1812 threatened Maryland. He was held by the British during the Battle of Baltimore after he went to the rescue of a captured friend.

### The Capture of William Beanes

The destruction of Washington, D.C. continued for two more days in August 1814, spreading from government buildings to private homes. Huge fires burned across the city, and flames were visible 50 miles (80 km) away in Baltimore.

As the British withdrew to ships on the Potomac River, a British patrol captured a local doctor, William Beanes. He was taken prisoner and was forced aboard the main British warship, *Tonnant*.

On August 30, militia officer Francis Scott Key learned of the capture of his friend Beanes. He went on horseback to Baltimore to locate Colonel John Skinner, the U.S. government official in charge of prisoner negotiations, hoping to persuade Skinner to sail down Chesapeake Bay to meet the British fleet and negotiate Beanes' release. On September 3, the two men set off in a **sloop**.

### The British Plan for Baltimore

Meanwhile, during the first week of September 1814, the large British fleet was sailing up Chesapeake Bay toward Baltimore. During the voyage, the British commander, General Robert Ross, and his staff finalized a two-part plan for a land and sea invasion of the city. The plan called for Ross to land several thousand men on North Point, a **peninsula** about 16 miles (25 km) south of the city.

**Settling Differences**

"All our differences with the Yankees will be shortly settled. This war cannot last long."

*British commander General Robert Ross, in a letter to his wife, September 10, 1814*

The sea-based attack, under the command of Admiral George Cockburn, called for British warships to bombard Fort McHenry. Taking the fort would allow Ross's troops a clear path into the city on land, and it would allow British warships to sail close enough to the center of Baltimore to bombard it.

## Fort McHenry

The fort that later became Fort McHenry was originally built as Fort Whetstone in 1776 during the American Revolution. It was far enough from Baltimore to protect the city without endangering it during battles. Whetstone Point, where the fort stood, was surrounded on three sides by water. This meant that enemy ships sailing into Baltimore Harbor would have to pass under the fort's guns.

The fort was built in the shape of a five-pointed star, with a deep, dry moat around the walls. The star shape prevented a direct troop assault on the walls and allowed defenders more opportunity to shoot at attackers. The stone structure that stands today was started in 1798 and finished in 1803. It was renamed Fort McHenry in honor of former secretary of war James McHenry. (McHenry's son, also named James, was an artillery officer at the fort during the battle in 1814.)

With the outbreak of the War of 1812, a series of improvements were made at Fort McHenry. The additions included a **battery** of cannons and new guns. The army also built hot shot furnaces, large brick ovens that heated cannonballs until they were red hot. The cannonballs were then fired at enemy ships to set them on fire.

An aerial view of Fort McHenry and the tip of Whetstone Point.

This map shows the sites of the Battle of North Point, the land-based conflict, and the Battle of Baltimore, in which British ships attacked Fort McHenry from the water.

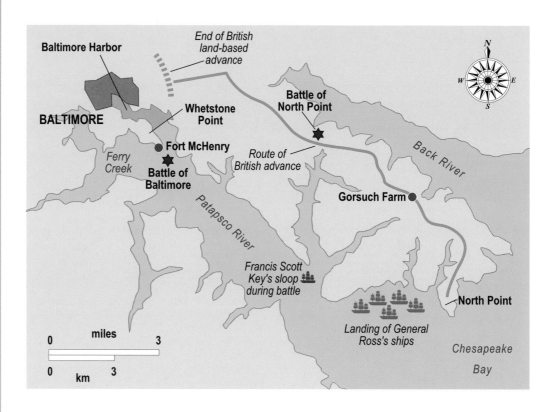

## Key Confronts the British

On September 7, Key and Skinner boarded the *Tonnant* to meet British commanders Ross and Cockburn. To make the case for Beanes's release, Key and Skinner produced letters from wounded British prisoners thanking Beanes for the care he had given them. This appeal convinced the British officers to release Beanes, but they would not permit the three Americans to leave immediately because they had learned too much about the **strategy** for the attack on Baltimore. They were placed under guard on their boat behind the British fleet to wait out the battle.

## The Battle of North Point

The battle on land, known as the Battle of North Point, began in a late summer rainstorm. On September 12, 1814, more than five thousand British troops landed at North Point and began the march northwest toward Baltimore. They soon encountered a small force of Americans who opened fire from the woods. When

General Ross rode to the front of the march to see what was causing the delay, a U.S. sniper's shot knocked him off his horse. The British commander died in minutes, and his blood-soaked horse galloped back through the shocked British troops.

The demoralized British pressed forward until they once again encountered enemy forces, at a place called Gorsuch Farm. After a short but intense fight, the Americans retreated. The British, however, suffered almost 350 **casualties**. They decided to camp for the night. They hoped that the shelling of Fort McHenry, which was soon to begin, would ease the way for them into the city.

## Treacherous Waters

The sea-based force, however, had also encountered obstacles. The water around Fort McHenry was too shallow to permit the largest British ships to come close enough to fire on the fort. To add to that problem, the Americans had sunk several ships in the passage

The Battle of North Point began badly for the British when their commander General Robert Ross was shot and killed. Things got no better, and the planned assault on Baltimore never took place.

into Baltimore Harbor, which made the approach even more treacherous. Admiral Cockburn was forced to attack Fort McHenry with a reduced fleet of sixteen warships, ten of which were just small gun ships.

### The British Open Fire

Key, Beanes, and Skinner were still under guard on their sloop about 8 miles (13 km) below Fort McHenry, when, shortly after sunrise on September 13, the British opened fire on the fort to begin the Battle of Baltimore. Inside Fort McHenry were about

## Fort McHenry's Flag

In June 1813, when Major George Armistead took command of Fort McHenry, he wrote a letter to the commander of the Baltimore militia. It read, "We, Sir, are ready at Fort McHenry to defend Baltimore against invading by the enemy. That is to say, we are ready except that we have no suitable **ensign** to display over the Star Fort, and it is my desire to have a flag so large that the British will have no difficulty in seeing it from a distance."

Mary Young Pickersgill, a flag maker in Baltimore, soon began work with help from her daughter and two nieces. The flag they made was so large that the women had to assemble it on the floor of a brewery. On August 19, 1813, Armistead was presented with a flag that measured 42 by 30 feet (13 by 9 meters)—about one-quarter the size of a basketball court. Each of the flag's fifteen stars was two feet (0.6 m) across.

This 1874 photo of the Star-Spangled Banner at Boston Navy Yard shows its huge size compared to the man standing in front of it.

one thousand men. From 2 miles (3 km) away, the British warships fired cannonballs, **Congreve rockets**, and mortar rounds (powder and shot-filled "bombs" that exploded after landing).

The intense shelling continued throughout the morning, with the British firing more than one shot a minute at the fort. Despite the barrage, most shells landed harmlessly because the British fire was so inaccurate. Luck was also on the U.S. side when a mortar round landed on the fort's gunpowder supply building but failed to explode.

## The Land Forces Approach

Meanwhile, the thunder of the British guns had alerted the land-based British troops that the attack was on. At about noon, the British forces marched into open fields several miles outside of Baltimore. There they encountered a huge force of Maryland militia, dug in behind **fortifications** on high ground.

This 1816 print by J. Bower is entitled " A View of the Bombardment of Fort McHenry."

33

British commanders were hoping that they could attack the city at the same time the British naval bombardment turned its guns from the fort to Baltimore itself. In the early afternoon, they tried a **flanking** attack to get around the enemy but were fought off. Later that night, they gave up and returned to North Point.

## The Long Bombardment

At about 2:00 P.M. on September 13, a British mortar round hit a cannon on the walls of the Fort McHenry, killing two Americans. Admiral Cockburn, believing that his direct hit had caused confusion within Fort McHenry, ordered his ships to close in on the fort. The British ships were immediately struck with intense return fire from the fort. Finally, the British ships were within range. Cockburn immediately retreated and resumed the long-range attack.

The British bombardment of Fort McHenry continued late into the evening without pause. At about midnight, Cockburn ordered

When the British moved in close on September 13, thinking Fort McHenry was vulnerable, the fort's cannons opened fire on the attacking ships. Cannons still perch on the walls of Fort McHenry today.

two of his ships to sail up Ferry Creek, a branch of Patapsco River, to attempt a flanking barrage. Early on the morning of September 14, however, the British ships were sunk by U.S. fire.

George Armistead became a national and local hero after his successful defense of Fort McHenry foiled British attempts to attack Baltimore. The city council of Baltimore commissioned this portrait of him in 1816.

## The Attack Fails

For twenty-five hours, as lightning flashed and rain fell, the British had bombarded the fort. The Americans inside, however, had stood their ground. By dawn, the British commanding officers realized that the attack on Baltimore would fail.

In less than two days, the British had lost General Robert Ross and suffered several hundred casualties. In addition, they had failed to take Fort McHenry and had lost two ships. At about 7:00 A.M. on September 14, the British ceased fire on Fort McHenry. The Battle of Baltimore was over.

Francis Scott Key catches sight of the U.S. flag still flying over Fort McHenry after the Battle of Baltimore.

## The Sight of the Flag

Down river, Francis Scott Key and his two companions had heard the thunderous barrage and imagined the worst for the U.S. defenders. But as their freed sloop sailed up the Patapsco River on September 14, Key saw the enormous U.S. flag flying over Fort McHenry. He began to write the words that would make him famous.

On September 17, as the last of the British fleet sailed toward the mouth of Chesapeake Bay, Key's poem "The Defense of Fort McHenry" was published. The poem immediately became so popular that its words were set to the music of a popular British song, "To Anacreon in Heaven." The result was the song known today as "The Star-Spangled Banner."

## Francis Scott Key (1779—1843)

Francis Scott Key was born in the western Maryland town of Frederick. He graduated from St. John's College in Annapolis at age seventeen, and by 1805 had set up a law practice in Georgetown, Maryland. In addition to his legal work, Key was deeply involved in the Episcopal Church in his town. As a pacifist, he opposed all wars. When the British sailed into Chesapeake Bay, however, Key volunteered to serve in the Georgetown Light Field Artillery militia unit, a position for which he had no training. After the war ended, Key served as a U.S. District Attorney and continued his religious activities, writing several hymns. He died on January 11, 1843, and was buried at Mount Olivet Cemetery in Frederick, Maryland. The U.S. flag flies over his tomb night and day, as it does at Fort McHenry.

**The Star-Spangled Banner**

"Oh, say can you see, by the
    dawn's early light,
What so proudly we hailed
    at the twilight's last gleaming?
Whose broad stripes and bright stars, through
    the perilous fight,
O'er the ramparts we watched, were so gallantly streaming?
And the rockets' red glare, the bombs bursting in air,
Gave proof through the night that our flag was still there.
O say, does that star-spangled banner yet wave
O'er the land of the free and the home of the brave?

"On the shore, dimly seen through the mists of the deep,
Where the foe's haughty host in dread silence reposes,
What is that which the breeze, o'er the towering steep,
As it fitfully blows, half conceals, half discloses?
Now it catches the gleam of the morning's first beam,
In full glory reflected now shines on the stream:
'Tis the star-spangled banner! O long may it wave
O'er the land of the free and the home of the brave.

"And where is that band who so vauntingly swore
That the havoc of war and the battle's confusion
A home and a country should leave us no more?
Their blood has wiped out their foul footstep's pollution.
No refuge could save the hireling and slave
From the terror of flight, or the gloom of the grave:
And the star-spangled banner in triumph doth wave
O'er the land of the free and the home of the brave.

"Oh! thus be it ever, when freemen shall stand
Between their loved homes and the war's desolation!
Blest with victory and peace, may the heaven-rescued land
Praise the Power that hath made and preserved us a nation.
Then conquer we must, when our cause it is just,
And this be our motto: "In God is our trust."
And the star-spangled banner in triumph shall wave
O'er the land of the free and the home of the brave!"

*Francis Scott Key, "The Defense of Fort McHenry," 1814*

Above is the
first verse of
"The Defense of
Fort McHenry"
in Francis Scott
Key's handwriting.
It is the earliest
known of Key's
handwritten drafts.

# Chapter 6

# The Final Months

The peace negotiations in Ghent, Belgium, shown here, went on for several months. **Delegates** argued about boundaries, shipping and fishing rights, and protection for Native Americans.

## A Peace Mission

While the Battle of Baltimore was unfolding, U.S. representatives were sailing to Ghent in Belgium to begin peace negotiations with Britain. They had left several weeks before Washington, D.C., was attacked. In the early 1800s, communications were so slow that the diplomats had no idea what was occurring in the United States as they sailed across the Atlantic.

The Americans were on a peace mission because the main issues that had sparked the War of 1812 no longer existed. The Orders in Council had been repealed in 1812. By 1814, another central issue, that of impressment, was no longer a problem either. The end of the war in Europe meant there were more than enough British sailors available to man British ships—thus, there was no need to take crew members from U.S. ships.

## Territorial Gains

The problem that remained, however, was that of the territorial gains made in the course of the War of 1812. The British had gained a foothold in the upper Michigan peninsula, and their position gave them control of the largest Great Lakes. With the war winding down, British military leaders in Canada had decided to press their advantage and try to gain control of the other Great Lakes, as well as Lake Champlain farther east (see the map on page 21).

## The Battle of Lake Champlain

The Battles of Plattsburg and Lake Champlain in New York, part of the British attempt to capture the Great Lakes, are considered by many historians to be the most decisive battles of the War of 1812. They took place at about the same time as the attack on Fort McHenry. In the late summer of 1814, a force of about ten thousand well-trained British soldiers under General George Prevost crossed into New York State from Canada. The British army moved down the western shore of Lake Champlain, forcing U.S. troops back to Plattsburg. At the same time, British warships under Captain George Downie moved slowly down the lake.

The Americans on land were outnumbered by three to one, but they had an excellent fighting force in their fleet on the lake, commanded by Thomas Macdonough. On September 12, under pressure from Prevost, the British fleet sailed into battle. Fifteen

In the Battle of Lake Champlain, the U.S. Navy once more proved itself surprisingly able to stand up to Britain's powerful Royal Navy. This print shows the tattered but victorious U.S. ships after the battle.

minutes into the fight, Downie was killed. The leaderless British fleet surrendered after some brutal **broadsides** from the U.S. fleet.

When he received word of the naval defeat, General Prevost called off his battle plan and retreated to Canada. The failed invasion ended British plans to take control of more U.S. territory.

### The Treaty of Ghent

By December 1814, peace negotiations were almost concluded in Belgium when news arrived of the British defeat at Lake Champlain. Suddenly, the U.S. position was strengthened. The United States refused to sign the treaty until the British agreed to withdraw from U.S. territory on the upper Michigan peninsula. The British agreed, and the Treaty of Ghent was signed on December 24, 1814.

## The Battle of New Orleans

Because communication was so slow across the Atlantic, one final battle was fought after the Treaty of Ghent was signed. It was, in fact, the largest battle of the war. In January 1815, U.S. General Andrew Jackson turned back an attack by British

U.S. forces turn back the British in the Battle of New Orleans.

forces at the Battle of New Orleans. The British suffered more than two thousand casualties, while the Americans lost fewer than a hundred men. When the U.S. Senate **ratified** the Treaty of Ghent on February 17, 1815, the timing of the treaty approval—following the victory at New Orleans— convinced many Americans that the United States had defeated Britain. In truth, the war had ended as a **stalemate**.

So the War of 1812 ended where it began, at least in terms of territory. The difference was that the Native American confederation that had sided with the British had been destroyed, and that left much of the territory in Indiana, Illinois, and Wisconsin open to white settlers.

## An Unusual War

In many ways, the War of 1812 was the most peculiar war in U.S. history. It began after one problem, the Orders in Council, had already been solved. It was not fought for the reason given—impressment of U.S. sailors—but rather to acquire territory in Canada, which was the basic aim of the War Hawks. The peace treaty did not give either side anything more than they had to begin with, and it addressed none of the problems that had caused the war in the first place. The largest battle was fought after the treaty had been signed, and the victory at New Orleans created the false impression that the United States had won a war that really had no victor.

A bulletin, published in Boston in February 1815, announces the news that a peace treaty had been signed several weeks earlier, ending the War of 1812.

### A Shocking Sight

"Of all the sights I ever witnessed, that . . . was . . . the most shocking. Within . . . a few hundred yards were gathered together nearly a thousand bodies, all of them arrayed in British uniforms. Not a single American was among them; all were English; and they were thrown by dozens into shallow holes, scarcely deep enough to furnish them with a slight covering of earth."

*British officer George Gleig, describing the scene after the Battle of New Orleans, January 1815*

## Evening Gazette Office,

Boston, Monday, 10, A.M.

The following most highly important handbill has just been issued from the Centinel press. We deem it a duty that we owe our Friends and the Public to assist in the prompt spread of the Glorious News.

## Treaty of PEACE signed and arrived.

Centinel Office, Feb. 13, 1815, 8 o'clock in the morning.

WE have this instant received in Thirty-two hours from New-York the following

## Great and Happy News!

### FOR THE PUBLIC.

To Benjamin Russell, Esq. Centinel-Office, Boston.
New-York, Feb. 11, 1815—Saturday Evening, 10 o'clock.

SIR—
I HASTEN to acquaint you, for the information of the Public, of the arrival here this afternoon of H. Br. M. sloop of war *Favorite*, in which has come passenger, Mr. Carroll, American Messenger, having in his possession

### A Treaty of Peace

Between this Country and Great-Britain, signed on the 26th December last.
Mr. Baker also is on board, as Agent for the British Government, the same who was formerly Charge des Affairs here.
Mr. Carroll reached town at eight o'clock this evening. He shewed to a friend of mine, who is acquainted with him, the pacquet containing the *Treaty*, and a London newspaper of the last date of December, announcing the signing of the Treaty.
It depends, however, as my friend observed, upon the act of the President to suspend hostilities on this side.
The gentleman left London the 2d Jan. The *Transit* had sailed previously from a port on the Continent.
This city is in a perfect uproar of joy, shouts, illuminations, &c. &c.
I have undertaken to send you this by Express—the rider engaging to deliver it by Eight o'clock on Monday morning. The expense will be 225 dollars :—If you can collect so much to indemnify me I will thank you to do so.
I am with respect, Sir, your obedient servant,
JONATHAN GOODHUE.

We most ardently felicitate our Country on this auspicious news, which may he relied on as wholly authentic—Centinel.

### PEACE EXTRA.

41

# Conclusion

Visitors to Fort McHenry can walk around the fortifications, imagining what it would have been like to be there as the bombs fell nearly two hundred years before.

## A Unified Nation

Despite its peculiar nature, the War of 1812—and in particular the defense of Fort McHenry—proved that U.S. military forces could stand up to one of the world's super-powers. Not only the U.S. Army and Navy, but some militia units had proved skilled enough to defend their land from a powerful invader. The United States would never again have to go to war with Britain over territory in North America.

## Fort McHenry Today

Since the War of 1812, Fort McHenry has never been attacked, but it continued to play a part in the coastal defense of the United States. A second story and a new battery with larger guns were added to the fort. It was used for training in the Mexican War of 1846–1848 and to house Confederate prisoners during the Civil War of 1861–1865. The military left Fort McHenry in 1912, and it was used as a hospital during and after World War I. After being restored by the U.S. Army, Fort McHenry was taken over by the National Park Service in 1933. As a national monument and the National Park Service's only historic shrine, it is visited by thousands of people every year.

The flag that flew over Fort McHenry had fifteen stars and fifteen stripes to represent the number of states (although there were actually eighteen states at the time). Later, the number of stripes on U.S. flags went back to the original thirteen, and just stars were added for new states. This famous flag is now in the National Museum of American History in Washington, D.C.

## The Legacy of the Writing of "The Star-Spangled Banner"

The timing of the U.S. victory at Fort McHenry, so soon after the nation's capital had been reduced to ashes, was important to U.S. morale. So was the fact that the Americans at the fort were able to withstand the onslaught of the most powerful navy in the world. It was a fine example to many Americans that they could stand up to Britain, and it was this resolve that created a renewed sense of patriotism that spread across the young nation.

One timeless example of that patriotic spirit was Key's song. "The Star-Spangled Banner" became enormously popular in the years immediately after its publication, and it was one of the favorite songs of Union troops during the Civil War. In 1931, Congress officially named "The Star-Spangled Banner" as the national anthem of the United States. The fact that the national song is about a flag, rather than any other element of the country, underlines the emotional attachment all Americans have to that symbol of the United States.

# Time Line

| | | |
|---|---|---|
| **1793** | ■ | Napoleonic Wars begin. |
| **1803** | ■ | Louisiana Purchase adds large territory to the United States. |
| **1803–1812** | ■ | British navy impresses more than ten thousand U.S. sailors. |
| **1807** | ■ | June: Three Americans are killed and eighteen wounded when USS *Chesapeake* is fired upon by British warship *Leopard*. |
| | | November: Britain passes Orders in Council prohibiting merchant ships from trading at French ports. |
| | | December 17: Napoleon issues Milan Decree, prohibiting compliance with Orders in Council. |
| | | December 22: Embargo Act becomes law. |
| **1809** | ■ | Embargo Act is repealed. |
| | | James Madison becomes president. |
| **1810** | ■ | May 1: Macon's Bill No. 2 is passed. |
| | | Napoleon deceives Madison into stopping trade with Britain. |
| **1811** | ■ | War Hawks press for invasion of Canada. |
| | | November 7: Battle of Tippecanoe. |
| **1812** | ■ | June 18: Madison asks Congress for declaration of war on Britain. |
| | | British capture U.S. forts at Detroit, Mackinac, and Dearborn. |
| **1813** | ■ | January 22: Battle of Frenchtown. |
| | | January 23: Raisin River Massacre. |
| | | April 27: Battle of York. |
| | | September 10: Battle of Lake Erie. |
| | | October 15: Tecumseh is killed at Battle of the Thames. |
| **1814** | ■ | March: Napoleonic Wars end with British victory. |
| | | Britain launches three-part invasion of the United States at Chesapeake Bay, Lake Champlain, and mouth of Mississippi River. |
| | | August 24: Battle of Bladensburg. |
| | | August 24–25: British forces burn Washington, D.C. |
| | | September 11: Battles of Plattsburg and Lake Champlain. |
| | | September 12: Battle of North Point. |
| | | September 13–14: U.S. forces defend Fort McHenry in Battle of Baltimore. |
| | | December 24: British and U.S. diplomats sign Treaty of Ghent in Belgium. |
| **1815** | ■ | January 8: U.S. forces defeat British army at the Battle of New Orleans. |
| | | February 17: Treaty of Ghent is approved by United States. |
| **1931** | ■ | "The Star-Spangled Banner" is adopted as U.S. national anthem. |

# Glossary

**artillery:** large, heavy guns, such as cannons.

**battery:** artillery unit of several guns.

**blockade:** blocking a port with ships to keep the enemy from going in or out.

**broadside:** firing of all the guns on one side of a warship at once.

**casualty:** soldier or other person who is killed, wounded, or missing in battle.

**confederation:** alliance of groups that agree to act together and support each other.

**Congreve rocket:** self-propelled missile carrying explosives.

**delegate:** person chosen to represent a group at a meeting or in making decisions.

**economic:** having to do with the economy, which is the system of producing and distributing goods and services.

**embargo:** ban on trade and transport of goods between one country and another.

**ensign:** symbol of nationality or power.

**estuary:** area of water where a river or rivers open out into the sea.

**flank:** side. A flanking attack means an attack from the side.

**fleet:** group of ships under a single command.

**foreign trade:** buying products from or selling products to another country.

**fortification:** structure built as protection from an enemy or in order to strengthen an existing structure for defense.

**frontier:** edge of something known or settled. The U.S. frontier moved west as white settlement expanded.

**merchant ships:** ships carrying cargoes of goods to be sold.

**militia:** group of citizens organized into an unofficial army (as opposed to an army of professional soldiers).

**Northwest:** part of the West in the early 1800s that was north of the Ohio River, now comprising Wisconsin, Michigan, Illinois, Indiana, and Ohio.

**Parliament:** British legislature (the part of government that makes laws).

**peninsula:** piece of land jutting out into water but connected to the mainland on one side.

**privateer:** privately owned warships that had government approval to attack and capture enemy merchant ships.

**ratify:** formally approve something by voting on it.

**repeal:** undo an earlier decision or law.

**shell:** case containing explosives, such as gunpowder, or other harmful material.

**sloop:** small, single-masted sailing vessel.

**stalemate:** conflict in which neither side can win.

**strategy:** plan of action.

**U.S. territory:** geographical area that belongs to and is governed by the United States but is not included in any states.

**West:** area of North America in the early 1800s between the original U.S. states and the Mississippi River.

# Further Information

## Books

Connell, Kate. *These Lands Are Ours: Tecumseh's Fight for the Old Northwest* (Stories of America). Raintree/Steck Vaughn, 1993.

Marquette, Scott. *War of 1812* (America at War). Rourke, 2002.

Maynard, Charles W. *Fort McHenry* (Famous Forts Throughout American History). Powerkids Press, 2003.

Pflueger, Lynda. *Dolley Madison: Courageous First Lady* (Historical American Biographies). Enslow, 1999.

Wills, Garry. *James Madison* (The American Presidents). Times Books, 2002.

## Web Sites

**www.americanhistory.si.edu/ssb** National Museum of American History, which houses the Star-Spangled Banner, has an online exhibition all about the flag, its history, and its restoration.

**www.nps.gov/fomc** National Park Service's web site has information about Fort McHenry National Monument together with historical information and maps of the fort.

**www.warof1812.ca** Canadian military heritage web site has documents, video clips, and articles about the War of 1812.

## Useful Addresses

**Fort McHenry National Monument and Historic Shrine**
National Park Service
End of East Fort Avenue
Baltimore, MD 21230
Telephone: (410) 962-4290

# Index

Page numbers in *italics* indicate maps and diagrams. Page numbers in **bold** indicate other illustrations.